Sexuality From A Rosicrucian

Viewpoint

Freeman B. Dowd

Kessinger Publishing's Rare Reprints

Thousands of Scarce and Hard-to-Find Books on These and other Subjects!

- Americana
- Ancient Mysteries
- Animals
- Anthropology
- Architecture
- Arts
- Astrology
- Bibliographies
- Biographies & Memoirs
- Body, Mind & Spirit
- Business & Investing
- Children & Young Adult
- Collectibles
- Comparative Religions
- Crafts & Hobbies
- Earth Sciences
- Education
- Ephemera
- Fiction
- Folklore
- Geography
- Health & Diet
- History
- Hobbies & Leisure
- Humor
- Illustrated Books
- Language & Culture
- Law
- Life Sciences
- Literature
- Medicine & Pharmacy
- Metaphysical
- Music
- Mystery & Crime
- Mythology
- Natural History
- Outdoor & Nature
- Philosophy
- Poetry
- Political Science
- Science
- Psychiatry & Psychology
- Reference
- Religion & Spiritualism
- Rhetoric
- Sacred Books
- Science Fiction
- Science & Technology
- Self-Help
- Social Sciences
- Symbolism
- Theatre & Drama
- Theology
- Travel & Explorations
- War & Military
- Women
- Yoga
- *Plus Much More!*

We kindly invite you to view our catalog list at:
http://www.kessinger.net

CHAPTER VII.

SEXUALITY.

NATURAL law is a safe guide in the range of being which is under law. Law is inexorable in the mineral, vegetable, and animal kingdoms, but in the human kingdom man has a measure of freedom. Of all creatures, he only is endowed with imagination and the power to originate. Animals look earthward, but the face of man, by some mysterious attraction, is lifted toward the heavens, and his horizon is practically unlimited. He sees pictures beyond the stars, never dreaming that he is gazing into the limitless vault of his own soul. There are no boundary lines to the realm of Imagination, in which man creates pictures, emotions, ecstasies of pain and pleasure, of hope and fear, of hatred and love. In this realm he discovers tastes that ruin and create habits, both above and beneath the laws of his physical being. The three lower kingdoms now organized into man's structure are as much subject to physical law as they were prior to such organization. In evolution, some new element is added at each step of progress. In the change of mineral to vegetable elements are found in the latter not possessed by the former and as the vegetable merges into animal there is developed the new element of volition, as if mind were added to clay. This, however, is only an appearance, for intelligence "sleeps in the mineral, dreams in the vegetable, wakes in the animal, and comes to consciousness in man." In the mineral, although only the intelligence of obedience, it is still of the same essence and akin to mind. Chemical affinity is the love of atoms, and in this love is generated the heat that throws lava from mountain tops and boiling water from geysers. It disintegrates minerals, softens the rock, and bursts forth in forms of use and beauty from the insensate soil. Evolution is only another name for Generation, and Generation is Sex Love. Sex Love is the action of the positive upon the negative principle, whether in inert matter or loftiest spirit. The love of the sun for the earth baptizes her with life and beauty, and this glory alternates with the shadowy night, with storm, winter, and decay. In nature, all things are male and female, and Evolution is the action and reaction of sex principles. If there is a condition of being wherein action and reaction do not exist, it is certainly an unknown condition. It is perhaps the conception of the Buddhist, but practically it remains a mental concept. So far as we know, motion co-exists with life ; the logical conclusion is that when motion has ceased nothing remains. Generation, working on many planes, producing different effects on each plane, is continuous in its operations, creating mental and spiritual as well as physical form and substance. Having fulfilled its office on one plane, it passes to another. To cease the generation of animal spirits by an abstemious diet with right mental attitude, is to begin the generation of spiritual force. Muscle is sometimes generated at the expense of mind. To cultivate one side of the nature without due regard to the harmony of the whole being, is to unbalance the entire economy inviting failure, weakness, and disease. Mind and muscle are both necessary in equilibrium, and it is a mistake to overbalance one side or the other. Habit, through long persistence, sometimes becomes second nature, the original true nature being overgrown and lost in the tangle of some unnatural practice revolting to those who view it from a more advanced condition.

Sexual habits contrary to nature are fatal, for sex has its roots in the soul itself. Animals have no evils of this nature, for they are governed wholly by the law of attraction. If the female invites the male, he responds; not otherwise. The female of the lower orders of life is as much bound by the law of expansion and contraction as the fruit tree, whose buds open and expand for the es.

cape of its spirit, and contract on the reception of its opposite, to produce fruit. The male is mastered by the female, but it is not the mastery of Will, or of physical force, or of the mind. We name it "instinct," and it is the attraction of the positive for the negative iron in the blood of each. The moment the negative is charged to fulness it becomes positive and repels, while the positive force becomes negative and quiescent.

The animal is simple, while man is complex. On the animal side, he is as little complex as are the animals, but on the mental side he is like a blooming flower, wide open to the influences from the universe of spirit, which, entering him in the form of thought and imagination, furnish to the blood and tissues something which the animal wholly lacks. By reason of this element he is master of himself and all lower life, if he wills to be master.

The field of Imagination is without limit and what a man adds to himself, lifting him above or sinking him below the brute, is of vast importance, for he creates it out of himself, — in fact it is himself in another form. Thus, as his creations are made up of the best of himself, he should consider well what he wishes to create before he becomes the victim of habits whose bondage he may be unable to throw off.

Habits involve the love nature. A habit of

accumulation generates a material love, a worship of material things that calls the soul downward toward the mineral and vegetable kingdoms, preparatory to reincarnation. That which we love we worship; it becomes our god and toward it we tend, for the soul's loves will become material by attraction to material things. Love is not an action, nor an object; it is that which prompts to action. Its weakest phase is desire of possession. Desire leads the mind and influences all action. The love of possession grows by the habit of getting. It soon becomes a monster never satisfied with accumulating and devouring material things, but fastens its vampire claws on the finest sensibilities and noblest attributes of the soul itself. When a habit is fully formed the soul is wedded to it and lost in the thing loved and labored for.

Sex love is nature's method of providing for the continuance of the race; but in excess it is like the instinct of the rat and the beaver which store up more than can be used. Those who do this tend downward; the creative power exhausts itself in excess and the mind reverts constantly to personal desires rather than to thought for the general good. The larger the mind, the more developed the will, the greater the power to control habits, passions, and desires. This control of self is one of the distinctions between man and the brute. By Memory and Imagination man is able to forecast the future and determine to some extent the consequences of his acts. Imagination is the parent of civilization, and inventions are not confined to mechanics. The governments, religions, social life, and loves are all products of man's prolific imagination.

Matter, under the law of repulsion, softens and expands and becomes more susceptible to the energizing influence of spirit, whether in the earth or in the human body. Soul which controls is so far removed in condition from matter that it requires an intermediate substance, or medium of activity, to enable it to establish intimate relations with matter. Mind is this vehicle, touching matter on one side and soul on the other. It is a pivot on which the man may turn in any direction a mirror in which to view himself; a telescope whose power is unlimited. The soul is "native and to the manner born" in a state of inconceivable bliss; its nature is pleasure, and anything that offers pleasure is attractive to it. Physical and mental nature are one. Moral and spiritual nature are also one. These two constitute man's duality. Matter is feminine, Mind is masculine; Morality feminine and Spirit masculine. For this reason God is termed *he*, although God is both masculine and feminine. The feminine in man's nature should receive the same care and education as should the masculine — equilibrium of these forces being necessary to sound health and longevity.

It has been affirmed that if properly generated man would not need regeneration. This is not true; generation in itself is perfect, because it is natural and without thought, while regeneration is the product of thought, which is not found greatly developed in the inferior animals. Thought that regenerates does not pertain to external things, but busies itself with God, duty, and the interior soul nature. These thoughts regenerate and build, cell by cell, the Divine Life within.

Sexual fire is generative; the same profound thought that stirs the emotions attracts this fire from the sex organs to the solar plexus, the central station of the soul — to burn on that altar until all grossness and lust are burned away, in the gradual transmutation of this mortal into immortality.

Thought is chemical, as it is mechanical, in its effects. It constructs, contracts, expands, and concentrates. It is the executive of the universe, but it is influenced by the Imagination, which leads thought to the depths and to the heights, to the far and near, to the unseen and unheard. Sexual fire is very sensitive to the action of thought and imagination; it glows and wavers and is fanned or quenched by their influence. It is this sensitiveness that gives the generative

power its intense actions and reactions ; the expansion of the atoms of the body influenced by
sexual emotion, enabling the soul to work therein
as it wills.

Excessive sexual desire is not the only form of
lust. There is the lust of dress, of display, of
wealth and power, for lust dwells in any excessive
desire for ownership. " Thou shalt not covet," to
own, or possess any thing, for the things we own
really possess us. They have taken possession
and we are obsessed by them in proportion to their
hold on us. Our children rule over us, our posses-
sions make slaves of us ; to save and hoard, or to
gather and scatter selfishly, absorbs our time and
best energies. The divine right of kings, the in-
fallibility of the Pope, private ownership of the
soil, all ownership, in fact, are assumptions born
of the imagination. When God takes anything
away from us the logical inference is that he is a
robber, if we really own anything. The fact is,
that we may use and enjoy anything we find in the
worlds of mind or matter ; but nothing possessed
or not possessed belongs to us. We brought
nothing into the world and we can take nothing
away.   •

The first work of Regeneration is to attain to
oneness, to unite the dual forces in yourself, that
as Jesus admonished " the eye may be single,"

seeing only God, who is Love, in all the universe
When that union is accomplished all things be
come lovely and lovable ; even discord helps on the
perfect harmony.   To attain this state, training o:
a specific character is necessary.   The externa
mind must be hushed into quiet ; the passions anc
animosities engendered by the friction of life must
be subdued before the Spirit can beget a child o:
God in the Soul.   The masculine and feminine
principles must be united in thought, motive, ob
ject and love.   This is purity.   The combinatior
of many things in agitation causes impurity; for
this reason the duality of Generation must give
place to oneness in Regeneration.   Man repre
sents spirit; therefore, Jesus called himself the
Son of Man.   Woman represents Matter ; wher
the violence of spirit is tamed, Matter and Spirit
unite and are one.

It is the masculine force that must be regener
ated in order to enter the kingdom of God.   Ir
the words of the Great Master, " Except *a man* be
born of water, and of the Spirit, he cannot enter
the kingdom of God."   All gestation is in water
and water is in matter as if in a womb.   Spirit is
that which impregnates and it is Matter alone that
becomes pregnant, for Matter is passive, negative,
feminine.   It is the masculine in each person that
must be regenerated.   To be born of water, the
male, (mind), must enter the feminine, (soul), for

these are the waters of life. To enter the soul is to enter into Love, and it is the office of the intelligence to find the soul and know the love, before full faith can be felt.

Love ranges from the lowest sensation to the ecstasy of angels: each thing that feels senses a degree of pleasure which takes rank in the consciousness as supreme. The highest physical sensation is the sexual generative sensation, which is the culmination of sex love. This culmination is the absorption of the positive by the negative and is only partial. That positive element which passes from the male is generally the vilest part, forced out by lasciviousness. The true feminine nature repels lasciviousness and consequently, instead of a free and natural blending of the two forces, there is antagonism which closes all avenues to Regeneration.

The spiritual being produced by Regeneration is first conceived as a germ in the male mind. As every person is *both* mind and soul — Mind being male and Soul female — the Mind must first find the Soul and gently blend with it. The new life, Regeneration, then begins in embryo, as a child in the womb. Love and the Soul are one and the quality of your love decides the character of the spiritual gestation. Unless the male principle in each nature enters *fully* into the Soul, there can be no spiritual gestation, by which it is perceived

that a divided *mind* cannot generate the Child
of God. "Ye cannot serve two masters." You
cannot enter into two or more diverse courses o
thought, conduct, or effort at the same time, fo
that is division; and a divided love cannot beget in
Regeneration. The man who loves two women
loves neither; he loves only himself. As he finds
nothing lovable, or rather attractive in himself
all the male elements being similars which repe
each other, he seizes on externals, and through
the imagination borrows that which attracts and
pleases—the most external and unreal of pleasures.

To attain to *oneness* of thought, the mind must
be focused on one desire with such intensity as to
cause a gentle heat to be felt in that nerve gang-
lion just above the back of the stomach, called
the solar plexus, which, as I have said, is the central station of the Soul. A single thought is a
sun-glass which being held to one point a suffi-
cient time, kindles a fire in things that obstruct
the light, until a hole is burned through dark matter to the source of light and heat. Well might
the poet sing :

"Come, Holy Spirit, Heavenly Dove,
    With all thy quickening powers,
  Kindle a flame of sacred love
    In these cold hearts of ours."

When this flame is kindled you *know* you have
a soul within ; the next effort is to get within it,

to blend and become one in mind and soul. When
in the soul, which is Love, you are in God, and in
time may be born of God; but the process of gestation is slow. In nature, growth is a slow process, and the growth of the immortal man is no
miracle, but follows the line of universal law.
This life is not for toil or pleasure, but for making
immortal all those who love it.

That which makes life a weary burden must be
cast aside; if in the mind only it must be re-
versed, turned back into the darkness of Chaos.
This reversal of hindrances and evils requires close
and vigilant attention; but this is culture of the
noblest faculties of the mind, will and desire; faculties that connect the mind closely with the soul
where God is. The Soul is the door to Infinitude;
through it the wandering mind is drawn to dwell
with, to become one with God.

Regeneration requires rigid and close analysis
of motive and desire, to the end that ONENESS may
be attained. If two natures appear, if two spirits
are within warring with each other, the call comes
to choose which you will serve, for the warfare re-
veals the preponderance of *force*, which belongs to
the plane of Generation. Force acts with violence, it *compels* obedience; but love gently leads
and persuades and attracts into the perfect life.
Force is hypnotic in its action, — it enslaves; but
love is freedom.

Sexual love is the love of objects. If the object to whom you give yourself in part make a like return, mutual satisfaction results and you are free to grow to the limit of that satisfaction. We are, however, so constituted that no two persons can follow the same line. Sooner or later the lines will so far diverge that the limit of satisfaction will be reached, and antagonism begin. It is apparent that sex love in its external manifestation is transient, ephemeral, belonging wholly to the plane of Generation ; while soul love is as enduring as the moral worth which attracts it, and is an element in the new man born of the spirit who has attained Regeneration. The love of objects is transient and barren, because the soul is never satisfied by objects, since no object can enter therein. No matter how many the objects loved, the soul, like a stomach fed on air, is always empty and hungry. Who can portray the burning thirst or the gnawing hunger of a loveless soul! A loveless soul is a sexless soul. Behold the world of mankind bathed in a sea of alcoholic drink to drown in universal intoxication, this immortal craving. See the mad rush for wealth and power, the incessant strife for place and position, the drunkenness of ambition, by which this hunger is partially appeased !

As already stated, to be born of God is to be born of Love ; and birth must presuppose a mother.

The Mother is nearest to the Father ; the newborn being must be born of the mother-love, that being the nearest approach to God. What words can express the immortal, imperishable character of mother-love! It surpasses all other manifestations of love. It holds within itself the potencies of all virtue. Beside its matchless supremacy, fame, gold and glory are so many worthless straws. The mother-love gives birth to the babe, and the soul of the woman is surrendered at the shrine of maternity. She is the providence of her offspring, its protector, guide and everlasting friend, with no thought of reward or desire of return in kind, being repaid fully by the love that warms her breast, and permeates her entire being. It is the mother-love that regenerates ; the true feminine love, — a creative and recreative force, into which the whole world can come regardless of ignorance, failure and sin.

Paul testifies to the transcendent worth of this powerful principle in the second chapter of Timothy, tenth verse, where he gives evidence of a knowledge that the mother-love was the true regenerative principle.

Christ is alluded to as "the only begotten son of the Father." Jesus said: "God is a Spirit"; therefore it is a truth that spirit begets children, or offspring. We know this, for nothing but spirit can enter into the womb. Spirit begets

love also, and various kinds of love are given
birth through varying environment, and the various
forms of spirit that beget, as for instance, a dom-
inating spirit begets self-love. This begetting
and birth is in each individual of the race, for we
are each one of us male and female. The spirit
is within, and from it is evolved the form, character and life conduct of the man, as from the invis-
ible emanates the visible. The marriage of a man
and a woman is merely an external expression of a
union already effected, and the child begotten of
that interior union is the materialized love, the
character of which is decided by the quality of
spirit predominating in each. Genuine marriage
is the union of the Father-Spirit with the Mother-
Love in each and every individual, and unless
such union is effected in each prior to wedlock,
there is no real marriage possible. The Father-
Spirit was referred to by Jesus as the Bridegroom;
and the Bride is the Virgin-Mother-Love that waits
the coming of the Bridegroom. The Christ is the
Only Begotten Son, born into the regenerated
man or woman from such union. Physical marriage is the external representation of spiritual
marriage, of this dual union in the nature of each
of the contracting parties; the failures and imper-
fections of marriage, therefore, are due to an im-
perfect spiritual union between the masculine and
feminine principles in each. The Christ is not be-

gotten because the Father has *not* descended to meet the Bride. Christ can only be begotten by the Father, and is therefore the only begotten Son of Love, — the saviour from sin and its consequence, — death. " Love lieth at the foundation "; it is the only life, the only immortality.

In order to know what manner of spirit is essential that one may make the conditions necessary to the evolution of the Christ, the nature of the Bridegroom must be explained and well understood.

CHAPTER VIII.

SEXUALITY (*Continued*).

THE Bridegroom is "the Father," so frequently spoken of by Jesus. He is the highest spirit that can manifest to man, or that can consciously enter into humanity. The Universal Spirit pervading all, which is all — the source alike of light and darkness, of good and evil, of pain and pleasure, of ignorance and intelligence, of virtue and vice — is *not* meant by this term, Father. The Father to whom Jesus constantly appealed is the Father only of the Christ. He is the Creator in humanity as differentiated from the Universal Creator. From him flows the seed of Regeneration and immortality, begetting the Christ in human nature — that "Word that was with God" and that "was God," declared by John. In the evolution of spiritual consciousness, he is the moving spirit appropriately styled the Bridegroom, whose Bride is the Divine Sophia of the Mystics; the Virgin mother-love of humanity.

Christ is a spirit, substantial, immortal, generated in every soul that desires him with the desire of Love; and *the growth of Christ in the human nature*

is Regeneration. ' No instantaneous transformation
is possible ; it is the slow growth the serious culture of a lifetime. It is a process, — conception,
gestation, and birth, infilling and transmuting every
atom of flesh into immortal substance. If "Christ
within you the hope of glory" means anything it
means immortality for *the entire man.* He who
aspires "to *know* of the truth of this doctrine"
must have the loftiest ideal conceivable of the
latent powers and possibilities of humanity.

Man's highest ideal of love is that which the
mother of his children manifests for him. Mother-
love is universal ; there is no conscious life void
of it. There is no weakness, defect, depravity, or
monstrosity to which she has given birth that is
outside of the mother's love and self-sacrifice. He
who can inspire this love in the breast of a woman
need ask for nothing more. If his nature is fine
enough to understand it and large enough to appropriate it, he has found Paradise.

The measure of a man is his ideal of woman.
It determines the loftiness of his flight or the
depth of his debasement. The mind of the true
bridegroom is ideal, filled with ardent devotion,
faith, trust, hope, confidence and anticipation.
His beloved is all the world to him ; without her
life itself would be a worthless show. The universe is full of her ; her breath is like the aroma
of flowers ; the touch of her hand transports him

to the verge of ecstasy. The glance of her eye kindles a fire in him that burns away all selfishness; for the time his feminine nature is supreme and he loses himself in love. Benevolence asserts itself, and he invites all the world to the marriage-feast, if it be only a crust. His pride of self is quenched and he becomes one with the universal. A taste of heaven is in this spiritual exaltation, and he might rise to still greater heights of ecstasy if his ideal were not ruthlessly torn from him by the contact of coarse, irresponsive matter with which ideals are clothed. This friction of matter is electrical in character; it has other objects to serve than merely procreation of the race. This is a Mystery and the key to it is held by woman. Instructed in this Mystery, she unlocks the door and brings man into wisdom and knowledge and power; ignorant, she drifts with him into disunion, disgust and despair. By possession of the being loved, without wisdom from her, he is cast out of heaven like Lucifer, Son of the Morning, the glorious being who had all things save love. So the bridegroom falls away from his loftier self; his idol is ·clay, something separate, apart from himself which he *owns*, not the beautiful spirit into which he fondly dreamed of losing himself in perfect love and rest. He has fallen back into *himself*, the material male spirit, which does not expand like the feminine to enclose all helpless things.

Love manifesting through sex acts on three planes: the Electrical, which has just been defined; the Magnetic, and the Ethereal. Of the last named we who are yet on the earth plane can know only from report—a glimpse caught by the clear eyes of some sensitive soul, or the vision of the seer, in deep sleep when the angels sometimes talk with men. Of the magnetic union it may be said that, like the birth of the Christ, it is potentially *possible* to all, but really known to only the few. The electrical union when *complete* and *perfect* gestates the spiritual body, atom by atom; the magnetic union regenerates it. It is attained through all-pervading Love; a mighty sea in which the Will rouses rhythmical, profound, searching vibrations. It is soul answering soul in the great deeps of Love, and the friction of matter plays no part in the ecstatic vibrations magnetically aroused. Here, too, the woman is supreme; but she must be pure of heart and sound of head; wise, too, with the wisdom of knowledge and experience, the woman

> —"nobly planned,
> To warn, to counsel, and command."

The higher we rise in the scale of being the less we need the friction of matter to produce creative vibrations, those vibrations on which God descends to become one with and in us.

He who would enter the woman soul in the magnetic union must be as fine and spiritual as that soul. The rough angles of his nature must be rounded off, his selfish arrogance be converted into gentle consideration for her and for others as his equals. The spirit of sacrifice and protecting care attracts love from the soul of the woman. Mother-love is a form of sex love, being its natural product. The two manifestations are alike in essence, having different objects. The man loses himself in the woman, while the woman loses herself in her children. The radius of a man's love is limited by the woman, but that of the woman, the mother, extends to many, and the more numerous the objects of her affection, the more expanded is her capacity to love.

It is the undifferentiated mother-love which returns good for evil and when smitten, turns the other cheek. When men are filled with this love, the Christ will be begotten in every child and Regeneration will begin in infancy. Feelings of tenderness and efforts to provide for and protect the weak are promptings of the Father, and the emanations from such a spirit promote friendship and attract love. Nay, more, they beget the Christ, the germ of immortality.

The desire to provide for the objects of love is prompted by the Father, but beware lest love cling to the *things* as well as to the objects loved. This is the divided love, the foe to that oneness which

alone begets the Christ. "Thou shalt have no
other gods " than love for Love's sake — but,
alas for the ideals of humanity ! Men and women
too often enter the married state simply for gain,
or worse still, for the gratification of sexual lust.
Right here woman has a mission. Her ideals of
attraction are false ; Marriage is the end, and dress
and ribbons, showy accomplishments, with *chic*, the
means. This gay display, this vanity of appearance, like fine feathers on the birds, may be one of
Nature's sly methods of perpetuating the race ; but
the majority of women would shrink from flaunting
such signals if they caught sight of Nature's inten-
tions.

Woman is a mystery, an enigma, — and this is
one of her most powerful attractions. We do not
desire that which we already have; we long for
something just beyond us, and an innocent co-
quetry is one of the feminine wiles to arouse and
keep active the masculine curiosity and longing.
"Pushed beyond its mark," it degenerates into
conscienceless deceit.

To appear more and better than we are is a
common aim. To overreach in trade, to get something for nothing, to get the better of a brother or
sister in any way, while preserving an appearance
of integrity and honor, affords the profoundest
satisfaction. To pervert innocence, to tempt the
lawless, to arouse passion by the display of false

charms, are but reflections from the debased ideals of mankind. The work of a spurious regeneration goes bravely on, and we see such born of water and the spirit daily by a profession of belief that Jesus of Nazareth is God, the Son of God, and a plunge in, or sprinkle of water!

Jesus could have used no more appropriate symbol in indicating the change in man from a mortal to an immortal being than the waters of birth, the fructifying generative water of the mysterious unknown, upon which the Spirit of God moved in the gestation of worlds and in which the embryotic child floats in its mother's womb, —water that quenches the fires that destroy, and which water the spirit is constantly impregnating with new forms of life. The new man is a new being, conceived by spirit, and gestated in the great deep of human nature to become possessed after birth, through the processes of growth, of power over the forces of nature, to be safe from hurtful or poisonous things, and able to defy disease and death. This it is to be "born of the spirit and of water." Plainly stated, the following are the conditions precedent to Regeneration : The masculine nature in man must know and enter into the feminine nature in himself. Thus out of the duality of Generation there will be established the oneness of Regeneration. The same action must take place in the nature of the woman. By the entrance of the male element into the female element of each individual, the Christ is *conceived.* Thought and desire turned inward to the permanent and spiritual, gestate the embryo, and its birth is the beginning of Regeneration. This work must be perfected in each individual *spiritually*, before it can appear physically, expressed in *character*.

Every man has within himself a mother-soul, or love, into which the mind must enter to be mingled with and assimilated before it is possible for him to attract the Bride, that Virgin mother-love which completes his divine nature by making him *one with the All.* In like manner the male nature in the woman must be blended with the female nature, which will then become Fatherly in character as well as Motherly. Justice and tenderness will be equal; the female expansiveness will become provident and the vacillating, ill-regulated Will becomes poised and regular in its action. The woman who regenerates the male elements in herself is self-reliant and self-governing, and no true man will aspire to rule over her. To govern herself is to govern her husband; and if her rule spring from wisdom, justice, and love, it will aid in his Regeneration. She can recreate him into what she herself has become in her male nature, by keeping her *ideal man* constantly in mind and living that ideal herself. The silent, persistent, *honest* thought-force of woman is irresistible, molding, fashioning, and controlling men, drawing them up to the heights of human nature and, alas! casting them down to its hells. She holds the keys to the kingdom of heaven both for herself and for man, for if she will take as husband only the man who represents her ideal of manhood, patiently waiting, fully expecting his advent into her life, *he will presently appear.* She must realize *intellectually*, that is, she must have in mind the complete picture of her ideal, as her soul *intuitively* knows him.

Undue sexual appetite, or lust, is due to an excess of animal magnetism, and a woman who has united the dual forces within herself can appropriate that magnetism in ways that will build anew the nervous system; but this power does not come by mere knowledge. It is a soul power, springing from love and command of the physical nature, which may be developed by intelligent training. A man thus controlled cannot help loving his wife devotedly, not *passionately*, but reverently, tenderly, purely.

Judgment and criticism of others has no legitimate place in those in whom the Christ is born. "I come not to judge the world, but to save it," is the distinguishing characteristic of the Christ. Man in the natural state judges others, but the Christ is Love, and not judgment. This Love throws the mantle of charity over the weaknesses and follies of the most depraved. In the words of our dear brother, John Heaney, the right spirit is expressed : " I believe that every one does *the best he can* under the circumstances he is in." That sentiment, affirmed by the judgment and exemplified in the daily life, evinces an exaltation of soul very far removed from the plane of ordinary human nature. The Inquisition, serfdom and slavery, together with all the wars and wrongs that blacken the pages of history, have sprung from man's presumption in sitting in the seat of judgment, that place which God only is competent to fill. He only knows the end from the beginning. He alone can see why poor humanity blunders and the wise keep silent before the injunction : " Let him who is *without sin* cast the first stone." If we feel the spirit of criticism rising within and words of reproach tremble on the tongue, let us take the matter "into the silence," and if we find the Christ within, judgment will give place to love, and the spirit of criticism will be swallowed up and lost in the Divine Wisdom. It is true that our intellectual judgment is for use ; but lest in our deficiency of wisdom we give premature expression of it where others are involved, let us learn to wait, watch, and pray, rather than blame another.

This is the end of this publication.

Any remaining blank pages are for our book binding
requirements and are blank on purpose.

To search thousands of interesting publications like this one,
please remember to visit our website at:

http://www.kessinger.net

CPSIA information can be obtained
at www.ICGtesting.com
Printed in the USA
LVHW022149011220
673139LV00050B/2449